BUG BUZZ

by Wayne Gerdtz

OXFORD
UNIVERSITY PRESS
AUSTRALIA & NEW ZEALAND

OXFORD
UNIVERSITY PRESS

Oxford University Press is a department of the University of Oxford.
It furthers the University's objective of excellence in research,
scholarship, and education by publishing worldwide. Oxford is a registered
trademark of Oxford University Press in the UK and in certain other countries.

Published in Australia by
Oxford University Press
Level 8, 737 Bourke Street, Docklands, Victoria 3008, Australia

ISBN 9780190317157

Series Editor: Nikki Gamble
Illustrations by Cat MacInnes
Designed by Oxford University Press in collaboration with Cristina Neri, Canary Graphic Design
Printed in Singapore by Markono Print Media Pte Ltd

*Links to third party websites are provided by Oxford in good faith and for information only.
Oxford disclaims any responsibility for the materials contained in any third party website
referenced in this work.*

Acknowledgements

The publishers would like to thank the following for the permission to reproduce
photographs: **pl**: Leena Robinson/Shutterstock; **p2/3**: Ian McKinnell/Getty Images;
p4/5 background: Hiroshi Higuchi/Getty Images; **p4l**: Stephen Dalton/Minden Pictures/Corbis;
p4r: Roland Bogush/Getty Images; **p5**: Peter Waters/Shutterstock; **p6**: Ed Reschke/Getty Images;
p7: Walter Myers/Science Photo Library; **p8l**: TeguhSantosa/Getty Images; **p8r**: Ian McKinnell/
Getty Images; **p9bl**: Danita Delimont/Getty Images; **p9r**: Jan Stromme/Getty Images;
p9tl: Minden Pictures/Masterfile; **p10l**: Papilio/Alamy; **p10r**: Marvin Dembinsky Photo
Associates/Alamy; **p11bl**: Don Johnston/Alamy; **p11br**: Thomas Kitchin & Victoria
Hurst/First Light/Corbis; **p11tl**: Sinclair Stammers/Science Photo Library;
p11tr/23: Rechtsanwalt/Shutterstock; **p12**: lauriek/Getty Images; **p13**: Fuse/Getty
Images; **p14**: Berndt Fischer/Getty Images; **p14/15**: Narinbg/Shutterstock;
p15: F1online digitale Bildagentur GmbH/Alamy; **p16**: Cisca Castelijns/ Foto Natura/
Minden Pictures/Corbis; **p17**: Leena Robinson/Shutterstock; **p18/19**: Scott Camazine/
Alamy; **p18l**: blickwinkel/Alamy; **p19r**: Stephen Dalton/Minden Pictures/Corbis;
p19t: Michael Durham/Minden Pictures/Corbis; **p20**: Ingo Arndt/Nature Picture
Library; **p21b**: Piotr Naskrecki/Minden Pictures/FLPA; **p21t**: karthik photography/
Getty Images; **p22l**: Rolf Nussbaumer Photography/Alamy; **p22r**: blickwinkel/Alamy;
p23b: Graphic Science/Alamy; **p23t**: StudioSmart/Shutterstock

Cover photo by blickwinkel/Alamy, back cover photo by Aleksey Stemmer/
Shutterstock

We have made every effort to trace and contact all copyright holders before
publication. If notified, the publisher will rectify any errors or omissions
at the earliest opportunity.

CONTENTS

FIND AN INSECT

Insects are everywhere – there are more insects than any other type of animal on Earth!

Some insects crawl or jump. Some insects fly.

All insects have:

one pair of antennae

a body that has three parts

six legs

a hard outer shell, called an exoskeleton

If you find an animal with all these body parts, you have found an insect!

5

INSECTS FROM LONG AGO

Insects have lived on Earth for a long time. Many insects were around even before the dinosaurs!

This insect **fossil** is more than 40 million years old!

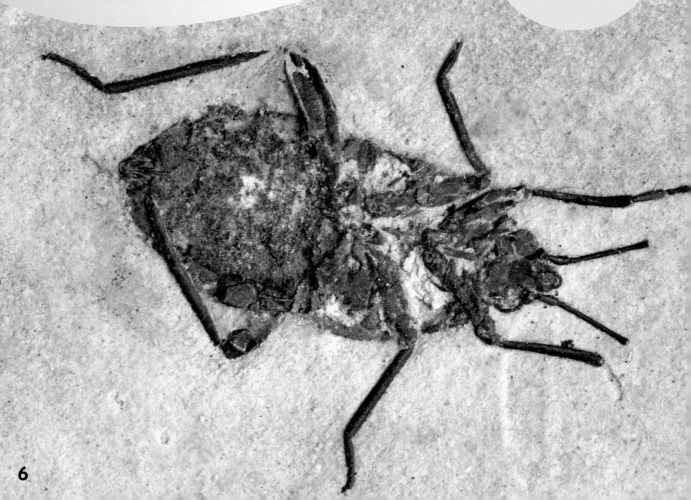

Millions of years ago, forests buzzed with insects. Some of them were *enormous*. Imagine a dragonfly as big as a duck!

INSECT HOMES

Insects live in many different places. Just like humans, they build their homes in places where they can find food.

lakes and rivers

hot deserts

snow-topped mountains

your home

rainforests

Scientists think there are millions of types of insects in rainforests that nobody has ever seen!

9

BABY INSECTS

All baby insects hatch from eggs.

Some baby insects look like little adult insects, such as these baby cockroaches.

Other baby insects look completely different from the adults. They go through big changes as they grow up.

baby cockroach

1. A butterfly starts life as a caterpillar in a small egg.

2. The caterpillar hatches from the egg … and it eats and eats.

adult cockroach

4. … into a butterfly.

3. The caterpillar becomes a chrysalis (*say* kriss-ah-liss) and starts changing …

SPECIAL EYES

Many insects have special eyes called compound eyes. Compound eyes are made up of many tiny parts – these are like lots of mini eyes.

Some insects have compound eyes that help them look at different things all at once. This means that insects can find food *and* look out for danger at the same time!

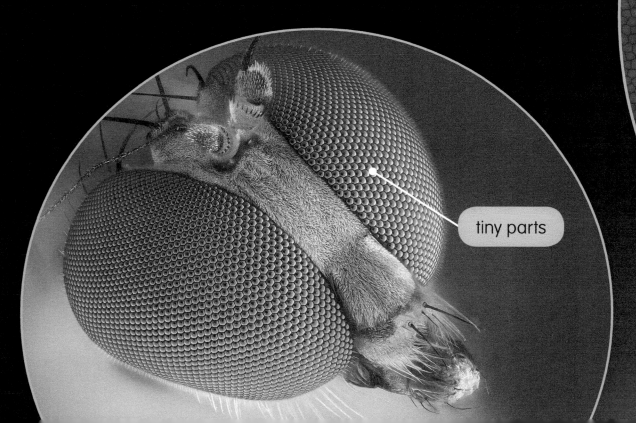

tiny parts

A flower looks very different through the eyes of a bee!

Each tiny part of an insect's eye sees something different!

AMAZING MOUTHS

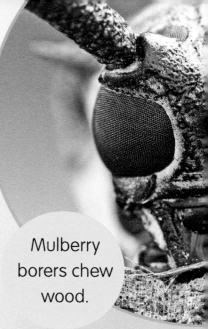

Insects don't have teeth! Instead, their mouths have special parts to help them eat. Each type of insect has different parts in its mouth, depending on the food it eats.

Mulberry borers chew wood.

Some insects have mouths that bite and chew.

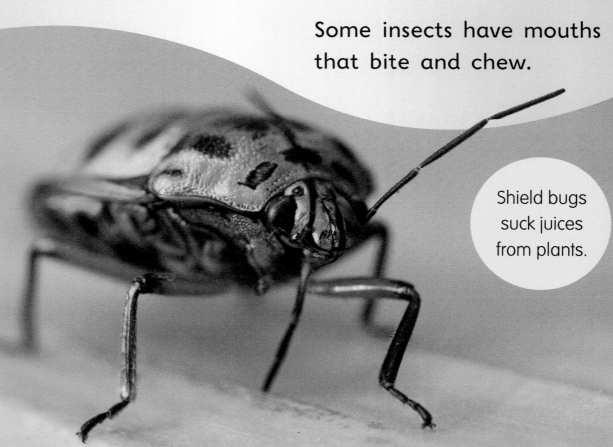

Shield bugs suck juices from plants.

Some have mouths that stab and suck.

Other insects have mouths that soak up food, just like a sponge!

Houseflies soak up their food.

15

WONDERFUL WINGS

Insects were the first flying animals on Earth. Most insects have four wings. Other insects, such as flies, only have two wings.

A dragonfly's wings are so thin that they are see-through.

Dragonflies have four long wings. This means they can fly very fast.

The patterns on this butterfly's wings warn predators that it tastes bad!

Butterflies have beautiful patterns on their wings. Sometimes these patterns help to protect the butterfly from **predators**. The patterns also help to **attract** other butterflies.

SIX SUPER LEGS

Insects have six legs, and each leg has six main parts. Insects use their legs to do different jobs such as burrowing, catching food, jumping and swimming.

Mole crickets use their strong front legs to dig.

The praying mantis has legs like hooks to hold its food.

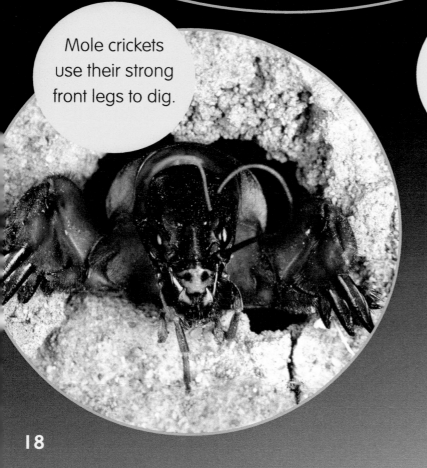

Grasshoppers use their long legs to jump away from predators.

Backswimmers have legs like paddles so they can swim across the water on their backs.

If a young stick insect loses a leg, it can grow a new one!

WEIRD AND WONDERFUL

There are lots of weird and wonderful insects all around the world.

Puss moth caterpillars make faces at predators to scare them away.

Treehoppers use their long, spiky horns to scare away predators.

The gladiator insect gets its name from its exoskeleton, which looks like **armour**.

WE NEED INSECTS

Even though some insects bite or sting, insects can also be very helpful.

Insects like bees, wasps and butterflies move pollen from flower to flower. This helps plants to grow new fruit and seeds for us to eat.

Baby insects, such as grubs, eat our food scraps.

This grub is eating a piece of old fruit.

Some insects make food that people like to eat – like honey, made by bees!

Some insects, such as ladybugs, eat pests that damage our plants.

So next time you tell an insect to buzz off, remember: *we need insects*!

GLOSSARY

armour: a tough outer layer to protect a soft body, such as metal armour worn in battle

attract: to draw attention

chrysalis: the hard outer shell on a moth or butterfly in the stage before it becomes an adult with wings

fossil: the hard remains of an animal or plant that lived millions of years ago

predators: animals that hunt other animals

INDEX